D1054496

Tips & Tricks
For Boomer Chicks

A Survival Book
For Retirement Years

Written and Illustrated
Gail Mewes

Introduction

My best friends and I used to spend our afternoons talking about all the wonderful things we were going to do *someday* when we retired. Calling ourselves the Boomer Chicks, much of the advice we came up with was good. Some of it was outrageous. Some was downright shameful. But all of it was aimed at preparing ourselves for the challenging golden years that lay ahead.

When two of our friends died from cancer, just six months apart, our little group fell apart. After a while, those of us who remained decided that the best way to honor our friends' memory was to actually *live* the rest of our lives the way they had wanted to, but never got the chance. So one of the "Chicks" went on a tiger safari to India and donated money to the Save The Tiger Foundation in our friends' names. Another joined the Peace Corps. Another got married. One by one, all the Chicks flew the coup. Until only I remained. So I decided to go on a six week trip down the Mississippi River in a foot pedal boat to raise money for cancer research. My family, of course, was horrified.

"There will be eddies and barges and snakes!" they cried. But I didn't listen. And when I survived, I sat down to write this book. Lucy, Marcie, Hedy and Pop, this is for *you*.

Part 1

Prepare Yourself *Mentally!*

*"I don't know why, Doc, but I've always felt
a little different, somehow."*

Change is inevitable. You could move
to a new home, or even a new state. You
might spend more, or less, time with your
immediate family or be thrown in with an
entirely new set of friends. You will have

different interests and social activities. You might even embark on a new career! Prepare yourself ahead of time for the challenges that lie ahead by strengthening your inner self with these Boomer Chick tips.

Avoid Those Psychic Vampires!

"Better turn up the thermostat, Dear. Aunt Gert is here."

Now is the time to focus on cultivating a positive, upbeat attitude about the future. Weed out the negative people in your life, the ones who focus only on all the *bad* things in the world. You know the type. They barge into your house without so much as a howdy-do, announcing, "The world sucks!...My boss sucks!...Men suck!..." On and on and on they will complain about their miserable lives without ever once asking how *you* are doing. Before you know it, you are just as depressed as they are!

No matter how much sympathy you give these types, they will always want more. Give them as much compassion as you can stand but limit your exposure to their doom and gloom. These people are psychic vampires who will suck every ounce of positivity out of you that they can.

Be True To Yourself!

"My wife went to one of those motivational speakers. Now she belly dances at senior centers."

A leopard can't change it's spots and neither can you. And why would you want to, anyway? There will never be another precious you! Be yourself. Stay true to your inner nature. Promise yourself *right now* that you will not live the rest of your life according to how others think you should live it. Embrace your wonderful personality, your unique good looks, your spiritual and political beliefs, your likes, your dislikes, and everything else that makes you...you. Be your own BFF and give yourself permission to enjoy the people and experiences that make *you* happy. As long as the things you enjoy don't harm anyone else, go for it!

Do Something Exciting!

Every once in a while, strengthen your inner fortitude by forcing yourself to do something a little scary. People who continue to do exciting things as they get older grow stronger, get their blood pumping and their minds off their troubles for awhile, all of which allows them to relax and have a more positive view of life. So go jump off a cliff, *literally!* If bungee-jumping or sky-diving seem a bit daunting, there are plenty of other things you can do that are exciting and exhilarating. When one of our Chicks turned 60 she went on a jungle excursion and had the time of her life. She got to stay in bamboo huts and go on moonlight swims under a waterfall. She even met someone with whom she had a brief jungle romance. Now *that's* exciting!

Talk To Yourself!

"Maybe she thinks it's a magic mirror!"

Positive affirmation tapes are wonderfully effective at drowning out the negative voices in your head. The best ones are the ones you make yourself! Studies show that affirmations you make for yourself are much more powerful than the kind you buy because our subconscious minds are more receptive to our own voices. Tailor your affirmations to your unique situations and record them against the background of soothing music. Then listen to your own soothing words while you are drifting off to sleep at night or after you have endured a particularly stressful event.

Believe in something!

"...and if you're the adventurous type, you can try the Religion Du jour Package. You'll be a Christian in one life, a Hindu in another, a pagan in the next, ..."

Research shows that people who believe in a higher power are more positive and well-balanced and exhibit a higher level of satisfaction with their lives. Even if you don't have a religious background, it couldn't hurt to examine the spiritual side of yourself. Become a religious explorer! Visit a church one month, a synagogue the next, a pagan gathering the next, and so on, until you find something that resonates with your unique philosophy of life. At the very least, you'll meet some interesting people. And, you never know, you just might find a spiritual home.

Take A *Mental* Vacation!

Need to get away but can't afford the time or money to travel right now? Take a mental vacation! Visualization is meditation with a bonus. According to best-selling authors like Rhonda Byrne, *The Secret*, it is possible to attract all sorts of amazing things to yourself simply by thinking happy thoughts! It works like this.

Go to a quite place and surround yourself with candles, pictures, music, scents, softly whirring fans and anything else that will remind you of the place you would like to visit. Once you have meditated yourself into a peaceful, relaxed state, just visualize yourself actually traveling to your destination and imagine how fabulous it will *feel* once you get there. That's all there is to it. Try to allow yourself at lease a half hour for your visualization "trip". Afterward, you will not only feel more relaxed and refreshed, but your dream vacation might be drawn to you like a cosmic magnet!

Allow Yourself To Have Fun

"Now get back down there, and this time learn how to have some fun, dammit!"

It's a sad fact that as we get older we often relegate ourselves to leading a life of "quiet dignity" (Translation: we turn into a stodgy old person). There is a little child in all of us who is just dying to come out and play but the voices in our heads (and, sometimes, coming from other people) tell us to "Act your age!" or "Don't make a fool of yourself!" Ignore those voices! They just stifle your natural urge to have fun. You have as much right to a good time as anyone else.

So, if you want to dance, *dance!* If you want to laugh, *laugh!* And if you want to bounce, *bounce!* My 82-year-old aunt still jumps around in bounce houses with her great-grandchildren. They love her for it and so does everyone else.

Conquer A Fear, *Any* Fear!

"It's the latest thing, a cellulite-sucking vampire bat!"

Conquering a life-long fear can be a
life-*altering* experience, especially if your
fear is deeply ingrained, such as a fear of
flying or of creepy critters (or of flying with
creepy critters!) It won't be easy, but if you
can face up to the thing that gives you
nightmares, the boost it will give your self
esteem and confidence will be enormous.

So pick a fear, any fear, and figure out how to conquer it (there are always ways to do it). You'll never look at life the same way!

Do Good To *Feel* Good

Volunteer Your GOD-GIVEN TALENTS!

"She was so moved by your sermon she offered to donate her 'services' to the sexually challenged."

No question about it, benevolence is good for the soul. It makes you feel good inside, too. Everyone has a skill or talent they can share. Even if yours is nothing more than your awesome ability to give someone your undivided attention and a great big hug, that one small act of kindness could make a huge difference in their life. It might even change it! Doing good shifts your focus away from your own problems and gives you a different perspective on life. It also reinforces the fact that you are a *good* person worthy of *good* things, which you are!

Still Depressed?

"And this one was caught trying to find her 'inner joy'."

Depression is a common complaint among people over the age of 50. Even if there is no obvious reason for your sadness, it can seem overwhelming, so treat yourself with as much sympathy, compassion and understanding as you would another human being. If your episodes of depression are chronically disabling, seek the counsel of a doctor or a therapist, but if your battles with "the miseries" are only occasional, the following quick fixes might help you feel better.

* **Plan something.** Whether it's a trip to the beach with your family or a movie date with your best friend, make sure you always have something fun to look forward to. It will lift your spirits every time you think about it.

* **Treat yourself.** Spend a few hours getting pampered in a spa, get a pedicure, try a new hairstyle, go to a movie. Everyone deserves a little pampering from now and then.

* **Change something.** Even the smallest change can shift your mood. I once lifted myself out of a devastating bout of depression by painting my kitchen bright yellow! Making even small changes forces your brain to think about something other than what you are depressed about and,

sometimes, that's all you need to snap out of whatever is bothering you.

* Start walking. Walking helps you beat depression in three ways: it gets you out of familiar surroundings that might be reminding you of the thing that is causing your depression, it activates endorphins to make you feel better, and it strengthens your body, which strengthens your mind.

* Try supplements. Recent studies have shown that depression can be alleviated by adding Omega-3 fatty acids, such as that which is found in fish oil and sardines, to your diet. Sam-E, available as a supplement in health food stores, also shows promise, as does folic acid, found in green vegetables, grains and beans.

* Get a hobby. Doing something as simple as needlepoint or quilting can help with depression. That's because the time you spend thinking about your hobby utilizes the left side (the planning side) of your brain, which gives the right side (your emotional side) a break. (Side note: It may also help you lose weight! Research has shown that if you do something like needlepoint or knitting while you watch TV at night you have much less chance of eating. So keep those projects handy!)

* **Pray!** It is a proven fact that praying releases a barrage of natural chemicals (endorphins) inside our brains and makes us feel better. Neurotheologists (yes, there is a field called that!) say it doesn't seem to matter how much we pray, what we pray for, or which entity we pray to, just the very act of praying makes us feel less alone and more hopeful about our lives in general. *Amen*

Part 2

Prepare Yourself *Physically*

*"Have a good time at the ball, but remember...
at midnight you go back into menopause."*

Your retirement years are bound to bring physical challenges, too, but the best part of your life doesn't have to be hampered by aches, pains and prescription drugs. By getting into the best shape you possibly can *now,* you will slow down the aging process and give yourself a head start, physically, so you can make the most of those exciting retirement years.

Get A Checkup!

"I hear he specializes in mood swings."

If you haven't had a checkup in awhile, now is the time to get one so you can find out what kind of shape you are currently in. Use that knowledge as a *starting point* to getting fit so you can make the most of your retirement years. The checkup doesn't have to be extensive. Just go to a clinic and have them check your weight, listen to your heart, take your blood pressure, test your urine for diabetes, stuff like that. Listen carefully to their recommendations but use common sense and *do your own research* if they suggest specific tests based strictly on your age. Remember, it is always your choice!

"Gimme all the remedies ya got, and make it snappy! I feel a really bad mood coming on."

Have you been in a bad mood lately? Are you having sleepless nights? Difficulty losing weight? If so, your body is probably rebelling against a dwindling supply of estrogen. It happens to every woman eventually. Hormone replacement therapy can make a huge difference in how you look and feel but you *don't* have to take

risky prescription drugs to give your body
what it wants. In fact, most of us do not.
There are natural remedies available today
that will ease your symptoms and help you
look and feel years younger.

Go Natural!

"I got yer Herb-al 'remedy' right here, Baby."

Speaking of herbal remedies, before taking prescription drugs for common ailments, try natural remedies *first*. Consult your doctor for serious health problems, of course, and consider any allergies you might have to the various herbal concoctions, but keep in mind that the less prescription medicines you take today, the better off your immune system will be in the future. Buy a book of home remedies to keep in your medicine cabinet and *use it*.

Find Clever Ways To Fit Exercise Into Your Day

"Since we've been jogging here, I've lost five pounds and learned a new language!"

Exercise tones the body, keeps the weight off, and fills your brain with those endorphin thingies that make you think happy thoughts. Unfortunately, it can also be quite boring. So find clever ways to work it into your daily routine. Jog home from work instead of drive, or park your car further away from your job or where you shop. Get an adjustable desk so you can stand up part of the time instead of always sitting down. Do your own gardening (if you like to garden), walk Poochie an extra block, run upstairs to use the bathroom and do jumping jacks during television commercials if you absolutely *must* watch TV. Soon, you'll be exercising more without even thinking about it. Your body will show it, too!

Get Some Sleep Already!

Nothing ruins your day like the lack of sleep. Crankiness, depression and weight gain are aggravated by fatigue so do whatever it takes to get a good night's rest. If your partner snores like a leaf blower, get a sound machine. Soothing white noise like ocean waves crashing against a tropical beach will drown out even the most obnoxious sounds. If that doesn't work, ask your doctor to hook them up with one of those electro-shock machines that gives them a small jolt whenever they begin snoring. Yes, it's a little mean, but knowing them, they'll sleep right through it!

Rev Up Your Love Life!

"And to ease your symptoms, I'm prescribing sex... every day...for the rest of your life."

Many women find it harder to fall asleep as they get older. If that's true for you, use those extra hours to your advantage! Studies show that having a love life dramatically reduces physical symptoms associated with aging and depleting hormones. Orgasm stimulates the production of estrogen, helps you lose weight and floods the body with endorphins that make you feel good all over. It also raises the body's level of immune-boosting antibodies, which keeps colds and flu at bay, and it's good for your heart, brain and digestive system. So, rather than toss and turn on those sleepless nights, grab your partner and do-se-do. What's that? You don't have a partner? Then do-se-do *yourself!*

How To Deal With Those 'Delicate' Situations

"Wow! We're way ahead. There must be a heck of a breeze today!"

At around the age of 50 or so, our digestive systems begin to process the food we eat differently, which can lead to embarrassing situations. Fortunately, wise Chicks know how to turn even the most unpleasant situation to their advantage. Their suggestion? Well, if you suddenly find yourself producing more natural gas than the Dakota flat lands, and your anti-gas tablets aren't working, just do like the big gas companies do—exploit it! Sit beside that snotty young thing at the next office meeting and let a quiet one fly. Just make sure your boss sees you roll your eyes and nod, ever so slightly, in her direction.

Get Fit By Learning Something New!

Have you ever wanted to learn how to tap dance? What about wind-surfing? Or ice skating? Or ballet? Your local YMCA or community college offers all kinds of fun things to do that won't cost you an arm and a leg and might even tone them up! You have a much greater chance of sticking with an exercise program if it involves learning a new skill. Not only will you have fun and meet new people, but learning something new will keep you interested in life.

Try Not To Worry

Finally, try not to worry. Worry puts a tremendous stress on your body. If you are frequently bombarded by stressful situations (or people!), try meditation, herbal supplements and relaxation tapes to help you relax and get back to your "happy place". There are all sorts of relaxation tapes available for everything from sleeplessness to nervous tension. You can even record them yourself. Just don't play them while driving!

Part 3

Prepare Your *Relationships*

"*I can't explain it, Aunt Dilla, but now that I've been through menopause, I TOTALLY understand where you're coming from.*"

Our personal relationships take on greater importance once we reach retirement age. Now is the time to improve your existing relationships, get closer to your friends, and make new ones!

Choose Your Friends *Carefully*

Robert Louis Stevenson said "a friend is a gift you give yourself." But choose your friendships carefully for they can affect your overall happiness as well as your financial circumstances!

Friends (including boyfriends) who only come around when they want something from you are called fowl-weather friends. When they only show up for the good times they are called fair-weather friends. Neither of these "friendships" are worth your time.

Friendships are a two-way street. If you suspect someone is using you (and you will know by the fact that *you* seem to be the one doing all the giving), consider cooling the relationship for awhile. Give them a chance to miss you. Hang, instead, with people who truly value you and know the meaning of give and take. You deserve to be with people who make *you* feel good, too!

Force Yourself To *Get Out There!*

*"...then we moved to Cornshuck...blah, blah, blah...
so I quit smoking and, boy, did I gain weight!...
blah, blah, blah...then my thyroid started acting up, and
you know how that is...blah, blah, blay...Hey! You should
meet my neice, she's quiet like you...blah, blah, blah..."*

Something as simple as a walk in the park can spark a new friendship. Many people move to new surroundings when they reach retirement age. It can be a lonely experience until you establish new friendships. It may seem a bit harder to make new friends as we get older, but it's definitely worth the effort to try, even if it is a little scary. The main thing is put yourself out there. Clubs, volunteer organizations and hobby classes are all good places to make new friends.

Reconnect With Family

"Isn't it nice how we've heard from so many new relatives since we won the lottery?"

 Being part of a tribe gives you a warm, fuzzy feeling inside. It will be especially comforting during your retirement years when, hopefully, you will be doing more traveling and more reconnecting with family. So send Uncle Ken a quick email to let him know that you've been thinking about him. Not only will it be fun catching up with what he's been up to, but it will give you a good feeling knowing that you can call on him the next time you happen to be in his neck of the woods. And that he can call on you, too!

Meet Family Obligations

"I don't know why she's making such a fuss over
Aunt Gert. She hasn't visited her in years!"

For the sake of family, we all have to
do things that make us feel uncomfortable
from time to time. Whether it's cleaning up
after your drooling ex-husband in the
mental hospital, squeezing yourself into
that metallic nightmare of a maid-of-honor
dress for your whiny, spoiled-brat third
cousin, or going to the funeral of that weird

53

aunt in Appalachia who used to chase you with snakes, meeting family obligations keeps you in the family loop and lets your family members know that you will always be there for them. That makes them a thousand times more likely to be there for you, too.

Forgive Them Their Trespasses,
But *Never* Forget!

"One last thing, Mom. Which of us do you really want to inherit your estate?"

It's hard to have a relationship with someone who has hurt you *unless you can forgive them.* Forgiving is not forgetting, however! Wisdom is learning how to compartmentalize past grievances in order to protect yourself in the future. For example, yes, you *should* forgive your sister for "accidentally" dropping her cigarette down your husband's pants on your wedding day just so she could fish it out. But think twice about inviting her to your next wedding. That doesn't mean you can't enjoy her feisty personality. Just enjoy it in small doses and *safe* settings.

Difficult Relatives

"...and the salad was dry, and the tea was weak, and the meat tasted like dingo dung! I WANT MY CIGARETTES!"

As the old saying goes, you can choose your friends, but you can't choose your relatives. Relatives are living proof that there is such a thing as karma. If you have good ones, good for you! As for some of the Boomer Chicks, to hear them tell it, Attila the Hun would fall weakly to his knees and grovel stupidly before the relatives that

57

God, in his infinite wisdom, chose to bestow upon them. They can only advise that you deal with them as best you can, with all the kindness and compassion you can muster. And if things do get out of hand, blame everything you say and do on your depleting hormones.

A Significant Other?

While many women prefer to be on their own, some long to be in a loving relationship. It's only human to want someone to go places with and share life's little experiences, like that giant electric bill you got last month. You might think finding the perfect mate after you've reached a certain age is impossible, but I'm here to tell you that it's not! I didn't meet, and subsequently marry, my sweetie pie until I was in my 40's. And while it wasn't my first marriage, it certainly felt like it was, complete with rainbows, starry nights and butterflies in my stomach. It still does!

It has been said that a woman over 40 is more likely to be hit by lightning than get married. Don't believe it! Men might fantasize about having sex with a 20-something bimbo, but most of them realize that if they want *real* companionship, someone with whom they can share their interests, who will love them for themselves and can talk about something other than what's on MTV, they'll be much happier if they stick to their own age group. So where are the best places to meet these fabulous boomer men? Well, the Boomer Chicks went a'hunting and here's what we found out.

1. Learn to play golf! If you are looking for a successful 'man of means' (doctor, lawyer, engineer, businessman type) learn to play golf! Guess what this type of man says is the number one thing he looks for in a woman (no...not big boobs). It's a smiling face! That's right! After years of competing in the dog-eat-dog world of business, doctoring, lawyering, or whatevering, this kind of man just wants to be able to relax and have a stress-free date with a good-natured, happy companion, *like you.*

2. Go to church! No kidding. Many women past 50 no longer enjoy the bar scene (if they ever did in the first place). If you are looking for someone for whom spirituality and family values are high on their priority list, try joining a church or synagogue. Many have singles meet-up groups which, according to my more pious cronies, are simply heavenly places to meet good men.

3. Join a veterans organization! Our war heroes appreciate encouragement and gratitude from warm, sympathetic women who understand the value of their bravery and sacrifice. Join a local USO or veterans organization if you have a hankering to meet a good-looking retired colonel with a take-charge attitude, a nice retirement plan and a kickass body.

4. Become an activist! Join a political group or volunteer to be a poll worker to meet men who are mother-country-and-apple-pie patriot types. Retired men often gravitate to politics hoping to make a real difference. You just might get caught up in their political 'passion'!

5. Take up dance! You would be truly amazed if you knew how many couples meet through square dancing clubs, but if square dancing is not your style, try joining a jitterbug club or my personal favorite, a good old-fashioned waltz club. Not only will dancing keep you in shape, but you might end up being swept off your feet by someone suave and debonair (sigh).

6. Take a night class! If you love learning, night classes are a fun way to meet and interact with men who share your interests. There are all kinds of classes, like gardening, computer classes and guitar playing, that appeal to both sexes. A quick search online or a call to your local community college will give you lots of ideas. You just might meet a nutty professor!

7. Go on guided tour vacations to fascinating places where real men like to go, like safaris or archeological digs. What's the worse that could happen? You meet a gorgeous Indiana Jones type? You lucky chick!

8. Volunteer for a civic organization! Historical societies are filled to the brim with civic-minded men who want to preserve their heritage. This type of man is usually athletic and likes to organize 10K runs, canoeing trips and other physically-challenging activities yet he won't mind going to a dress ball, either, if it promotes civic pride. What a guy!

9. Take a hike! Hikes and similar outings

are loads of fun and are a great way to meet active men. This type of man enjoys getting physical but he also appreciates Mother Earth and our natural surroundings. Hiking is a good way for you to stay in shape, too. There are hiking clubs, like the Sierra Club, that organize hiking trips to beautiful places all over the world. How romantic!

10. Get a dog! Walking a dog is, by far, the cheapest and easiest way to meet people of the opposite sex. Men love dogs and they like talking about their dogs. The doggies love the exercise, too. Parks, hiking trails and even outdoor restaurants that allow Poochie will give you the opportunity to strike up a conversation with other canine lovers. And if you have a fancy schmancy pooch, consider entering him or her in a dog show. (Just don't go all *Best In Show* on us!)

As you can see, the Chicks had lots of tips on how to find love in all the *right* places. And most of them came from personal experience. You will notice, however, that online dating services and bars did not make the list. That's because most of my cronies (including me) are paranoid about meeting strangers online or in bars. But if you are braver than us, and if you <u>swear to God</u> that you will be super careful, even that might be your cup of tea. (And there's yet another idea—visit a tea house. Maybe you'll meet a dapper English gent!)

Already in a relationship? Great! But if it is less than perfect, the following suggestions might help you strengthen it. Retirement is not the time to spend your days duking it out in a hellish battle of wills.

Don't Hold Grudges!

"Honeybunch, are you sure this is good for my prostate?"

The Boomer Chicks' No. 1 tip for maintaining a good relationship with your significant other is to *not* hold grudges. Hanging onto a grudge is useless. All it does is make you all tense and bitchy inside. Besides, your resentment is bound to sneak out in subtle ways. But, trust us, sprinkling itching powder in his shorts will never endear him to you in the long run. It's better to get your emotions out in the open and let him know how you feel. Even if he doesn't actually validate your feelings (a typical man-thing), at least he'll know where you stand. And that will make *you* feel better, at least.

Focus On The Friendship Side
Of Your Relationship

One of the main reasons couples stay together in their golden years is companionship. As people age, and they face new health issues, it becomes increasingly important to have each others' backs during the good times as well as the bad. Known as the "us against the world"

phenomena, it is comforting to have a relationship with someone who comes from the same era and shares similar politics, values and *music*.

Deal With Your Anger *Constructively*

"I'll be right there, Sweetums."

If your partner occasionally ticks you off (and whose doesn't?), find constructive ways to deal with your anger. Fighting rarely brings good results long-term. Instead, channel that negative energy into doing something positive *for yourself* that will calm *you* down and give you an emotional break. Get away from the other person for awhile and take a brisk walk, do a high-powered aerobic workout or go on a pleasant outing with friends. Once your anger has been spent, you'll be better able to think about the situation rationally, and it is within your rational mind where solutions to problems are born.

Make Plans Together

"Hon, you know that romantic vacation you're always talking about? Well, guess what I bought!"

Nothing brings couples together like making plans. It's always uplifting to have something to look forward to. Whether it's a cruise, a weekend at a luxury resort, or a cross country trip in an old RV, planning for something that you both look forward to is one of the most enjoyable things you can do as a couple. It will give you

something to talk about when you are
cuddling under the covers at night, and
whisper about when you are with others.

Try To Understand Your Partner's Point Of View

"Group, welcome our latest member. He survived his wife's menopause a few years ago and still wakes up screaming."

Try to remember that you are not the only one going through challenging physical and mental changes. Your mate is probably dealing with stuff, too. Only recently have doctors agreed that there really is such a thing as "male menopause". Of course, it's not nearly as hellish as what

we Chicks have to endure, but it's
something to consider, nonetheless.

If All Else Fails...

"When I count to three, you'll wake up, and whenever your wife rings this bell you'll say, 'Yes, Dear...whatever you say, Dear.'"

Have you tried everything you can think of to put the old spark back in your relationship but still can't seem to get it together? Well, there's always couples counseling. All couples go through rough patches. A few counseling sessions might remind you why you got together in the first place and put your relationship back on track. If you do decide to go that route, look for a counselor who has lots of experience in couples therapy, and make sure they are understanding, sympathetic and impartial. But, above all, make sure it is someone *you* choose. It never hurts to stack the odds in your favor! *Just kidding!*

When To Dump A Relationship

"Helen, I don't think this is what your therapist meant when she told you to dump him."

It's impossible to get along with everybody. If a friend or family member is causing you misery, first try to resolve your differences with a mediator. Even if you live far apart, you can find a professional mediator on the internet who will counsel you through the phone or via a conference call. You owe it to yourself to at least *try* to salvage the relationship, especially if it is an important one. But if it is unlikely that the two of you will ever see eye-to-eye, you just might have to end the relationship for awhile to save your sanity. Even so, try to leave the door open to a possible future reconciliation. People can change, you know.

Part 4

Prepare Your *Finances*

"I don't care if rich Uncle Shamis is senile, his dying wish is to leave his millions to a showgirl, so tonight you're a showgirl, dammit!"

Retirement is looming! Even if you have a nice pension and some Social Security waiting for you, unless you are a millionaire, there will inevitably be financial challenges once you have to live

81

on a fixed income. You'll sleep better knowing that you are preparing for them ahead of time.

Set *Attainable* Financial Goals

"She can't come in to work today...she's too exhausted from setting goals."

Set realistic, *attainable* financial goals. Start by cutting back on your household expenses and brainstorm ways to add to your income with either a part time job or business once you retire. Dedicate a separate calendar to your goals and every time you meet one, mark it on the calendar and reward yourself. Not only will it serve as a record of your accomplishments, it will motivate you to keep going. By preparing for your finances ahead of time, you will get into the right mindset for sticking to a budget and stay focused and on track. And *that* will make your financial future seem a lot less scary.

Go After That Raise *NOW!*

"Why, hello Mrs. Peabody. Mr. Peabody is in conference, right now, but I'll have him call you back after he and I have a little meeting."

Nothing quite lifts one's spirits like a little extra money in the old bank account. Even if you really love your job, it will be even more rewarding if you are fairly compensated. It will also go a long way toward reaching your retirement financial goals. Unfortunately, most bosses have a knee jerk reaction when it comes to handing out raises. It's called the "No-way-in-hell" response. It works like this.

When asked for a raise, the first thing many bosses say is, "No way in hell!" followed by a million excuses why they can't give you a raise at this particular time (the economy sucks, the company is being audited—blah, blah, blah). Here's what to do:

If your boss says no to your request for a raise, look disappointed and remain silent for a moment or two (count to a minimum of ten), then say, "That's very bad news... [pause]...well, then, is it OK if I take a longer lunch break today?" That will get his attention! Now he knows that you are really, really serious about that raise thing. Since he's already feeling bad for nixing your raise in the first place (bosses are only human, you know) he'll probably say yes to the longer lunch, but even if he says no he'll spend the rest of the day wondering what the heck you are up to and if you have decided to pursue other opportunities.

The fact is, no boss ever wants to lose a good employee. Bosses hate problems as much as anyone else does. They know that if an employee quits they'll have to actually *do* something about it. They also know that it will probably cost them twice as much to train a new employee than give an existing employee a well-deserved raise. So, chances are, once your boss has time to think it over, if you have been a good employee, he'll get back to you with some kind of an offer. When he does, it will probably go something like this...

"I'll have to check with corporate first (which is pure BS because 'corporate' really doesn't care as long as the job gets done), but I might be able to give you a 1% raise."

If you are happy with the 1%, take it. If not, prolong your boss's agony a bit longer by saying you were "really hoping for a little more".

The key to successful negotiations with a boss is to hold out for as much as you think you are worth on the open market. That is something that only a good long talk with yourself can tell you. You might get a 5%, or even a 10% raise (10% is usually the max). In the end, dickering with your boss is a little like playing poker. Just make sure you are holding all the cards before you call his bluff!

Network! Network! Network!

"All I know is, things haven't been the same around here since she joined that New Age group."

Networking, online and off, opens the door to all sorts of possibilities. Should you decide to write a book or start a business or find a part time job to help grow your retirement nest egg, networking with others who share similar interests can bring you tons of prospects, sales and business connections. You'll also have fun and make interesting friends along the way!

Get That Promotion!

"Sir, before I send in the auditor, have you given any more thought to my promotion?"

Now is also the time to get proactive about that promotion you've had your eye on! Promotions usually come with pay increases which will ultimately effect your retirement benefits. Talk to your boss asap and remind him how hard you have worked for that promotion and how good you would be at the new job. Give him a list of your accomplishments and show him your *documented records* proving all the extra hours you worked late without ever once complaining. If that doesn't work, drop a few hints that you know *every single one* of the company's juicy little secrets!

Update Your Skills

"Amazingly, these techniques are still considered effective today."

No matter what kind of job or business you decide to tackle in your retirement years, take advantage of any extra skills that you can acquire *now* to pad your resume. If you are currently employed, check with your HR department to see if your company offers free courses in computer skills or management. Not only will it make you a more valued employee to your current employer, but it will look good on your resume should you decide to apply for any future jobs.

Manage Your Time Wisely

"I'm thinking, I'm thinking!"

Time is money. Distractions, procrastination and poor time management will sabotage your best efforts to reach your retirement goals, but for little more than it costs to go out to dinner and a movie you can hire an accountant who will not only keep track of your finances but will soothe your nerves at tax time. A good financial adviser is worth his or her weight in gold, *literally*. Just be sure to check out their credentials thoroughly before you hire them. Smart Chicks don't take chances with their money or their honey!

Volunteer!

"Like, alls you have to do is take this little eel dude door-to-door and find it a good home."

Believe it or not, one of the best ways to make new business contacts is to volunteer. Even if you only have an hour or two a month to spare, donating your skills to a worthy organization can reap major benefits in terms of increasing your business and social network. In fact, many companies routinely look for qualified *paid* workers among their unpaid volunteers. It only makes sense. They figure if a person works for their organization for free, they will make the best employees, too. And, on a personal level, volunteering also makes you feel good!

Recruit Friends And Family

"Now this is a little technique I like to call 'walking the dog'."

Now is the time to call in all those favors! Recruit all the friends and family members that *you* have helped over the years so they can help you in your quest for financial freedom. Aunt Lola can coach you on how to make extra $$$ in a home party business, Cousin Timmie can put flyers up in his hardware store to advertise it, and your sister can spread the word about those adorable leashes you'll be selling. Make a list of everyone in your family (at least the ones you are still speaking to) who *owes you* and try to think up ways they can help.

Part 5

How To Look Good, Even When You Feel Like Crap

Every women knows that when you look good, you *feel* good. If the days are gone when you can get up in the morning, throw on a little lip gloss, run a brush through your hair, and dash out the door looking great, well...join the club! We are all riding *that* train to hell. Still, you never know what exciting thing retirement years are going to throw at you, so the Chicks had the following tips for keeping you looking your very best, no matter what.

Don't Get Stuck A Time Warp!

"Trust me, ladies. This look is all the rage in Beverly Hills."

Lets be honest. Being stuck in the past dates you. Mullet hairdos, overly plucked eyebrows and bright blue eyeshadow is out, at least for *this* decade. If you are caught in a time warp, and a good hard look in the mirror (or a brutally honest friend) will tell you if you are, it's time to say goodbye to your past and get back to the future. To find out what's trending in makeup and clothes for your age group just turn on the TV. Stylish actresses spend millions keeping up with the latest. Find one whose age, body type and coloring is similar to yours and take notes. What works for them will work for you, too!

Use Your Wardrobe *Subliminally!*

Advertisers know that colors have an almost mystical effect on people. Used correctly, they can subliminally influence the mind and motivate people to think a certain way and even buy stuff! Here is a crash course to help you choose wardrobe colors that will give you the subliminal edge the next time you go out on a "girls night out". Pink says "Maybe I will."; Red says "I *definitely* will!", Blue says "I won't tell if you won't", Yellow says "Let's have fun!", Black says, "Okay, but I'm in charge", White says, "Forget it. I'm a virgin and I'm gonna stay that way."

Magic Cures For Puffy Eyes

Puffy eyes are a common problem as we age and they can make you look years older. That's because, as our skin gets thinner, so does the membrane that ordinarily holds back fat in the upper and lower eyelids. As the membrane thins, the fat herniates and pushes forward, which causes bulges to form under the eye. Not to fear! The Boomer Chicks had some excellent tips for getting rid of the 'puffies':

1. Mix your own "shrinking cream" by combining Witch Hazel half-and-half with Aloe Vera gel (do a patch test if you think you might be allergic to Aloe Vera). Store the mixture in a jar in the refrigerator and _be sure to label it so no one eats it!_ (This actually happened to the husband of one of the Chicks) Apply the cream under your eyes and blot off any excess. Do not get any in your eyes!

2. Keep foundation makeup in the refrigerator, too. When applied cold, it will help shrink puffiness (and large pores).

3. Never eat salty foods after 5 pm! Salt causes water retention and is a major cause of puffy eyes and jowls in the morning.

4. Elevate your head slightly when sleeping.

Note: *Some* people swear by using hemorrhoid ointment under the jaw line to eliminate a double chin. *Some* people even say it works to shrink puffiness under the eyes. The Chicks can't recommend this particular treatment because hemorrhoid ointments contain chemicals that might harm your eyes if it gets into them. In any case, we just wanted you to know what *some* people are saying. As always, use your own judgment.

Makeup Do's And Don'ts

"Is it just me or did Helen go a little heavy on her makeup tonight?"

Makeup is the finishing touch we put on the face we present to the world. Ironically, the older we get, the less makeup we should use. Beauty experts (and the Boomer Chicks) suggest that we stick to light foundation, a little blush, a hint of eye shadow, mascara, and one of those long-lasting lipsticks. And they absolutely forbid *ever* going to bed with makeup on! Nighttime is the only chance your skin has to renew itself. Treat it to a good cleansing, some nourishing moisturizer and a little facial massage to stimulate collagen production. You'll thank us in the morning!

Splurge!

"I know we're at the wrong Tony's but this guy knows his stuff!"

Consult a professional to find out which makeup and colors are best for your particular hair and skin type. And don't skimp on the cost! A good makeup consultant will save you tons of money on future purchases because they'll eliminate all the guesswork and you won't waste money on stuff you'll just end up throwing away (yes, we've all been there!) And practice putting on your makeup *fast* so you can be ready for anything at a moment's notice. My southern granny used to say that a lady should be able to put on her makeup in under 3 minutes flat. "You just never know when them Yankees will be comin'." And she oughta know. She married one!

The Natural Way To Luscious Locks

Thick, shiny hair is the hallmark of youth and vitality. Invest in a great haircut that will give your hair lots of bounce and highlights. Treat it gently and avoid over-teasing it or using harsh sprays and chemicals on it. If your hair has begun to thin (a common problem as we get older), here's a *natural* conditioner that you can easily make in your kitchen using Aloe Vera, the plant that is often used in expensive products to make hair thicker and stimulate new growth.

Mix fresh Aloe Vera gel, either from a plant you grow or the kind you buy in health food stores, half-and-half with your favorite hair conditioner. Do a patch test first if you think you might be allergic to Aloe Vera (rare). Use your new conditioner after every shampoo and you should see a noticeable difference in the thickness and shine of your hair within a month! All the Boomer Chicks swear by it.

Stimulate Your...er...*Complexion*

"Are you sure he specializes in _facial_ massage?"

One night, as one of the Boomer Chicks was flipping through her TV channels, she came across a movie star touting the benefits of her facial massager. It seems that her expensive little vibrating gadget could massage away wrinkles and improve the texture and firmness of one's complexion. Well, naturally, the Chick had to try this! So she ran and got her own little vibrating gadget (she insists it was her *back* massager, ladies!) and set it to work on her face while she watched the rest of the infomercial. Sure enough, twenty minutes later her skin glowed like a new baby's bottom! After she passed this little tidbit of information along to her fellow Chicks, we went to work doing research and discovered that facial massage really does increase the blood supply to the skin, which stimulates the production of collagen, which improves skin tone! Who knew? So, did any of us ever purchase the movie star's expensive gadget? Nope. Our...er...*back* massagers get the job done just fine.

Nips And Tucks, Anyone?

A little cosmetic surgery never hurt anybody. Well, that's not *exactly* true, but if you shop around for an accredited plastic surgeon and get references, there's certainly no harm in treating yourself to a little 'nip and tuck' every once in awhile. The Boomer Chicks all agree, if you can afford it, *go for it*. It will certainly lift your spirits (among other things). Just don't overdo it. You don't want to end up with your eyebrows where your widow's peak oughta be!

Camouflage, It's Not Just For The Military Anymore!

The only difference between how others perceive how we look and how we *really* look under our clothes is how cleverly we have learned how to conceal our problem areas. All of us have them, but using the right color, fabrics and styles can camouflage our imperfections and emphasize our assets. For example, if you want a certain part of your body to look slimmer, drape it in dark colors and use solid colored fabrics or patterns with small prints while avoiding bulky knits, bright colors and shiny fabrics. To make something look bigger, accentuate it with light, bright colors and bold prints and use strategically-placed scarves, jewelry or belts to draw the eye to your best features.

If you want your feet to look smaller, wear wedges or heels (they don't have to be really high heels) in matte fabrics and darker colors. And, unless you have elf feet, avoid pointy toe shoes like the plague. If you like to wear open-toed sandals, paint those toes! Everyone notices toes... *everyone. E*specially men. They might not say so, but they do. Paint them with red or pink polish or treat yourself to a pedicure and get "french toes". *Ooh la la!*

Get Some Perspective!

"Hmmmph. You ask me, she ain't a day over 69!"

We all need an ego-boost from time to time. If your self-esteem has taken a hit lately, you can give it an instant lift by hanging around with people who are much older than you. *Seriously!* By the time someone is in their eighties or nineties, they are no longer so concerned about how young they look. What matters most to them is how young they *feel*. So volunteer at a senior center or some other place where seniors hang out. They will inspire you to keep your priorities in order. Sure, they'll talk your ear off with stories about the "good old days", but they'll also call you "youngun" and tell you they wish they had skin like yours. Compliments like that are guaranteed to make you feel younger than springtime!

Part 6

The Boomer Chicks' Top Ten Commandments

"I'm glad I ran into you, Reverend. The wife and I were just planning a quiet evening at home."

The Boomer Chicks thought the following suggestions were so important they called them their *commandments!*

Thou Shalt Not Linger Over Grievous Images!

"Don't ask."

One day, as I was washing my windows, I happened to spot my neighbor, Gus, weeding his rutabagas. As he bent over and tugged at each reluctant weed, I saw his trousers slip ever lower on his massive frame until they threatened to reveal his hairy horror. Now, you might well ask, why didn't you just shut your eyes and walk away? But, I tell you, had I been watching an alien abduction, I could not have been more transfixed. So there I remained, for long minutes, awaiting the inevitable, which, when it came, turned out to be much less entertaining than expected.

Ever since, I have been on the lookout for pointless mood busters that gobble up the precious minutes we have each day to spend on stuff that will *truly* bring us joy. So turn off those depressing news shows that assure us daily that the world is going to erupt into chaos at any moment. Unless there is something you can actually *do* about it (like vote!), it is pointless to dwell on it. Focus, instead, on making your own little corner of the world a happy place for yourself and others. Let the rest of the world take care of itself. It will, anyway.

Thou Shalt *Never* Stop Learning!

"We like to think of ourselves as progressive here at I.O.U. One of our programs even allows you to plan your curriculum around your mood swings!"

Learning keeps your braincells young! Within our small group, every one of us Chicks is in the process of learning something new. One Chick is taking a business class, another is going after her real estate license, another is taking a quilting class. I am learning how to speak Spanish. The old notion that learning gets more difficult as you get older is pure nonsense. It is a proven fact that the very act of learning exercises the brain and helps ward off dementia and other brain-related diseases associated with aging. So go learn something!

Thou Shall Tryeth Strange New Things!

"HA! I told you this trip would be a waste of time!"

Retirement is the time to try new things and explore all those things you've been just dying to explore but never had the time. Like looking for Bigfoot! Really! There are scads if special interest groups out there that go on backpacking trips in search of Sasquatch, Nessy, UFOs and other strange things. Mostly, the members just end up sitting around a campfire getting soused on Hellbat Tequila and telling tall tales, but just imagine how exciting it would be to actually find one of those things! Now *that* would be a story to tell the grandkids!

Waste Not Thy Children, Nay, Nor Thy Children's Children!

"Guess what, Mommy! Grandma taught me a new game! It's called 'Little Princess Dust Mop'!"

Speaking of grandchildren (or grandneices and grandnephews), retirement is the perfect time to bond with those little munchkins. But don't wear yourself out in the process! The best gift you can give them is a sense of responsibility, so along with home baked cookies, give them chores! Children love playing games. A clever grandma will invent games that both she and her grandchild will enjoy—games like "There-is-a-monster-hiding-under-your-bed-that-can-only-be-banished-if-the-floor-has-been-vacuumed-by-a-child". Of course, once they become teenagers they will consider themselves too cool to play with Grandma. That's when a game of "I-have-hidden-the-car-keys-amidst-all-the-clutter-in-your-room-and-you-won't-find-them-until-you-clean-it-up" will come in mighty handy.

Thou Shalt Not Cooketh Thy Noodle, But *Useth* It, Instead!

"It's a Thanksgiving theme party! We pretend to be the starving pilgrims and you bring the turkey, Cousin Sharon brings the bread, Uncle Eddie brings the wine..."

If you are the one who has been doing all the planning, shopping and cooking for holidays and family gatherings for umpteen years, it's time to let someone else do the work. Use your noodle and turn the reigns over to the younger generation. It is time for *you* to relax and enjoy yourself. You've certainly earned it!

Thou Shalt Not Covet Thy Neighbor's Ass, Nay, Nor His *Gardener's* Ass!

"Since hiring Sven, the view of our garden has improved immensely."

Do you envy your neighbor's beautiful Asturias? Does your mouth water when his roses bloom bigger than cabbages while yours whither away on the vine? Many Boomer Chicks like to garden once they reach retirement age, and gardening *is* great exercise, but if you absolutely hate to garden, and if money is too tight to hire a gardener, consult the bulletin board of your local college. You'll find lots of ambitious, bronze horticulture majors who will be more than happy to pamper your posies for a reasonable fee. A beautiful garden of flowers and herbs will lift your spirits and can save you money by supplementing your food source!

Take Not The Name Of Thy Cleaning Lady In Vain!

"We like to match our Happy Maids with the preferences of our clients. So if you could tell me exactly what you have in mind..."

Wouldn't it be great to have a live-in housekeeper? Alas, most of us can only afford one in our dreams. But we can still treat ourselves to a cleaning *service* occasionally if we are frugal with our budget. Cleaning services save us time so we can do the things we *really* enjoy. They

stuff we normally forget about,
ıg fan blades, kitchen appliances,
ıroom faucets.

our budget is tight, consider joining one of those skill pools that are cropping up all over the country. As baby boomers become the most populated segment of our society, people with all sorts of work skills, like ex-plumbers, ex-bookkeepers, and ex-house cleaners are organizing skill pools to...well...pool their skills! So dive in! It works like this. When you join a skill pool, you trade a couple of hours of *your* skills in exchange for someone else's. No money exchanges hands. One of our Boomer Chicks trades her cooking and catering skills for all sorts of other services in her skill pool. If you can't find a skill pool in your community, *start one* among your Boomer Chick friends.

Thou Shall Have No (Unwanted) House Guests Before Thee!

"Did you get the feeling we should have called first?"

There is a time and a place for socializing. People who habitually "drop by for a visit" because they think you have lots of time now that you have retired can put a real kink in your plans. Not to mention, it's just plain rude. Your good friends already know you well enough to know that you prefer that they call first before showing up on your doorstep (except in emergencies, of course). But, if there are still some in your circle who think nothing of dropping by whenever they take a notion, have a heart-to-heart talk with them and ask them to please, please, *please* call ahead first. That way, you can be ready for them when they arrive and entertain them in style!

Thou Shalt Not Waste Thy Time Trying To Fix Other People!

"Welcome to Schleppford Retirement Village! We are the Schleppford Wives Welcoming Committee...the Schleppford Wives Welcoming Committee...the Schleppford Wives Welcoming Committee...the..."

Are you one of those people who are always taking on everyone else's problems in the mistaken belief that you can actually fix them? Well, stop it at once, Missy! You can't fix other people and they will only resent you if you try. If someone close to you has mental or emotional problems,

143

treat them with as much compassion as you can, then refer them to a professional who can actually help them. Alcoholics, drug addicts, obsessive Schleppford wife types and other self-sabotagers will only drain you of your own precious energy and stress you out. In the end, they are the only ones who can really fix their lives, anyway. But you knew that already, didn't you?

Taketh Thyself On A Yearly Sabbatical

"Welcome back, Madam. Taking another 'sabbatical', are we?"

I was surprised to learn how many of the Chicks like to go off by themselves from time to time to renew their spirit. One has developed her "sabbaticals" to a fine art. Once a week, she empties her purse into a jar marked "My Getaway Fund", and by the end of the year, she has saved up enough to...get away! So she makes arrangements with her family to be gone for a few days, clears her calendar, packs some good books, comfortable clothing, candles, herbal teas, comfort food, and anything else that strikes her fancy, and off she goes! Only her family members and a few close friends know where she is and they are under strict orders not to contact her unless there is an absolute emergency.

One year she went to Sedona, Arizona, to live with a Native American tribe for a week and learn about herbal healing. Another time she went on a New Age cruise to the Yucatan Peninsula where she explored centuries-old pyramids and studied ancient Mayan culture. Another time she spent Halloween in Salem, Massachusetts, learning about the witch persecutions (and a little magic, besides). She has traveled to Vermont to learn how to make maple syrup, been on a crystal-hunting expedition in the Ozarks, hiked in the Black Forest with the Sierra Club, and once she went on a snorkeling treasure hunt off the coast of Florida.

Needless to say, her adventures have been nothing short of inspirational to the rest of us. She never reveals *exactly* what she does on her sabbaticals but she always comes back grinning like the Cheshire Cat and sporting a brand new optimism about life. She says she goes on her sabbaticals alone because it challenges her and forces her to take risks that she otherwise wouldn't dream of taking, and *that* keeps her young at heart!

Part 7

Finally, Be Prepared For Those "Special" Situations!

"I picked them up on Global Warming Code #315, Sarge...having hot flashes in a restricted zone."

    Along with all the good things our retirement years bring, there will also be unique problems and challenges that are age-specific. Let's face it. It can be a harsh world out there. We need to be ready to cope with it! The following hypothetical situations may seem extreme, and some of the Chicks' suggestions may seem downright shameful, but we figured, if you can handle these problems, you can survive *anything* your retirement years throw at you!

Operation "Meltdown"
How to turn a weakness into a strength

"I HAD to give her a refund. She was going into meltdown!"

When our bodies betray us it can make for some embarrassing situations. But take a tip from the Boomer Chicks. If you can figure out a way to turn a handicap into an advantage, you will come out ahead in *any* situation.

The Situation: You are in a hurry to beat the afternoon traffic and buy an expensive dress without bothering to try it on first, only to get it home and discover that it is way too small for you and not your best color! When you try to return it the next day you are confronted by a snotty salesgirl who tells you that there will be no refund! You get so upset you feel an embarrassing hot flash coming on! *What do you do?*

The Plan: Don't argue with that impossible wench. Use that hot flash to your advantage! Clutch your chest and pretend to gasp for air while you mention that your doctor warned you not to get "overly excited". Then ask to speak to the manager so you can get the name of the store's attorney. Odds are, you'll get that refund, my friend!

Operation "Big Mama"
How to handle a bully

"But, Tiffany dear, it IS your size. It says so right there on the tag. Maybe if you just suck in a bit..."

Bullies come in all shapes, sizes and ages. The most obnoxious type is the person who thinks *they* will never gain weight or grow old. They love reminding you of *your* age and anything else they consider *your* flaws, however. Don't let them get away with embarrassing you in front of others. Get tough!

The Situation: It's time for the Secret Santa party and you happen to draw the name of your boss's favorite secretary, that skinny bee-och who is always making nasty comments about your weight. Your boss will be at the party so you have to get her something nice! *What do you do?*

The Plan: Buy her a pretty sweater! In fact, buy two sweaters—one in the size she is always bragging about, and a second, identical, sweater two sizes smaller. Carefully remove the tags from both and sew the tag from the sweater in her size onto the smaller sweater. When she opens it at the party, insist that she try it on!

Operation "Dead Weight"
Learn how to multitask!

"Great reception! And that Aunt Ida is
quite the listener!"

No matter how organized you are, or
how well you try to plan for things, the
unexpected can rear its head when you
least expect it and cause problems, *unless*
you know how to multitask!

The Situation: Oh no, Aunt Ida has

kicked the bucket! You had promised her that you would host her memorial service but your daughter's wedding happens to be the very same day! You can't possibly be in both places at the same time, can you? *Or can you?*

The Plan: Aunt Ida loved her Celtic heritage so throw her a good old-fashioned Irish wake! Dress her up in her finest and prop her up in the reception line at the wedding. It was what she would have wanted, after all!

Operation "Exterminator"
How to deal with pests

"Like I TOLD ya, Lady, we don't do PEOPLE!"

Of course, some problems (like weird relatives) will just follow you into your golden years. Be prepared with an arsenal of clever ways to deal with them.

The Situation: You throw a party and your drunken brother-in-law shows up unannounced, threatening to spoil everything.

The Plan: Tell that looney-tune that one of your guests has lost a diamond earring in your backyard. If he finds it, he'll get a big reward! When he staggers outside to look for the treasure, toss a bottle of Jack Daniels after him and bolt the door. That oughta keep him busy for awhile. Now your guests can have a good time and you won't be embarrassed by his antics.

Operation "Cookie Monster"
How to be resourceful under pressure!

"The club is here to pick up your "homemade" cookies for the bake sale."

It's only natural to want to make a good impression when moving to a new location or joining a new club. The pressure will be on you to be helpful and charming. But you must also be *resourceful*.

The Situation: You join a fancy

schmancy club and are anxious to make a good first impression, but at your first meeting you are told that everyone MUST contribute something homemade to the annual bake sale which will take place the very next day! *What do you do?*

The Plan: Agree to contribute 6 dozen frosted sugar cookies and enjoy the murmurs of approval from the other members. After the meeting, dash to the grocery store and buy some canned frosting and 7 dozen sugar cookies from the bakery (you will eat one dozen as a reward for being so clever). That night, frost the cookies and arrange them on a pretty platter. At the bake sale, whenever someone asks you for the recipe, just smile and tell them it's a "family secret".

Operation "Rug Rats"
How to handle thoughtless impositions.

"Of course, I'll babysit! We just joined a hunt club. The kids can help us clean our guns!"

Once you retire, there will inevitably be those who see your new found freedom as an opportunity to impose on your time. Be prepared beforehand so you can stop them in their tracks.

The Situation: You have a horrible

migraine. All you want to do is lie on the couch with a cool rag on your head and sip Bordeaux until it goes away. Suddenly, you see your neighbor coming up the walk, the one who is always asking you to babysit her hellions for "just a couple of hours, since you now have so much extra time". *What do you do?*

The Plan: Grab the fake rifle you keep behind your front door (you do keep a fake rifle behind your front door, don't you?) Open the door and tell your neighbor that you would be happy to watch her little ones. In fact, they can help you clean your guns!

Operation "Bless You!"
How to prepare for the inevitable

"I wonder why Aunt Gert's allergies kicked in."

Ideally, your retirement will be a stress-free time to enjoy quiet evenings at home. But you know, better than anyone else, that *some* situations will continue to annoy you even after you reach your golden years. In fact, they may even get worse!

The Situation: It's your wedding anniversary. Candles are glowing, soft music is playing and his Viagra is starting to work. All of a sudden, the doorbell rings. It's Aunt Gert! She has pulled this sort of stunt before but you don't want to send her away angry. After all, you are in her will! But you and your sweetie have been planning this evening for weeks. *What do you do?*

The Plan: This time you are ready for your aunt's shenanigans. Knowing she has an allergy to animal dander, you quickly retrieve your stash of feline hair and scatter it about the room. Within minutes the poor dear erupts into fits of sneezing and retreats, leaving you and your honey bunch to resume your romantic evening.

Operation "Oops!"
How to protect your personal space

"Be careful when you serve the passenger in 6A. She seems a little 'accident prone'."

    Wouldn't it be great if we could just wipe out life's little annoyances with a mere wave of our hand? Impossible, you say? Well, the Boomer Chicks know of at least one situation where that would actually work!

The Situation: You are on a long flight

and your seatmate is a burping, farting creep who wants to talk the entire time (when he's not burping or farting, that is). *What do you do?*

The Plan: You should already know that the odds of sitting next to a bozo on a long flight are ginormous, so mentally prepare yourself ahead of time for what you must do. Once the flight is underway, order a Bloody Mary. When the flight attendant delivers it, wave your hand in animated conversation and 'accidentally' spill the mess all over your seatmate. It's next to impossible to remove Bloody Mary stains so when he goes to the bathroom to clean it up, he'll be there for awhile. Enjoy your flight!

Operation "Shake Up"
How *not* to be taken for granted!

"*And for an extra $1,000 we can give you a Mona Lisa smile and Bette Davis eyes!*"

You love the people in your life but sometimes they are clueless to the fact that you have needs, too. If you do all the giving and no one seems to want to give back, maybe it's time to shake 'em up a bit!

The Situation: You have been feeling unappreciated lately. Your family is driving you crazy and you would like to do something drastic to get their attention. *What do you do?*

The Plan: (You will probably have to save up for this one but it's worth it!) Instead of checking yourself into a nut house, go to a nice resort and focus on yourself! Get a complete makeover—hair, makeup, clothes, the works. When the "new you" returns home, it will show your family that you are still full of surprises. They'll think twice about taking you for granted in the future!

Operation "Bait And Switch"
How to get what you want!

"Well...I asked for a Mercedes, but I 'settled' for THIS!"

This might seem a bit sneaky, but retail stores do it all the time to make buyers *think* they are getting a good deal. Right before a sale, they'll raise the prices on items so when they go on sale customers will think they are getting a real bargain.

The Situation: Your birthday is coming up and your husband/boyfriend/partner asks you what you want. You have your heart set on a diamond tennis bracelet but you know your sweetie will only say, "Sorry, Darlin', my huntin' dawg needs a new jacket". Dang! You really wanted that bracelet, too! *What do you do?*

The Plan: Ask for something ten times more expensive than the bracelet, like a new car! When he says no (which, of course, he will because...duh, it's a *new car!*), look crestfallen and say, "Well, I also kinda wanted a diamond tennis bracelet, too..." That bracelet doesn't sound so expensive, now, does it? Wear it in style!

Operation "Fresh Start"
Because smart Boomer Chicks *always* have a
good backup plan!

"And she lived happily ever after...well...mostly."

In the end, no matter how much you
want your retirement years to be the best
years of your life, or how hard you try to
make it happen, sometimes life will
blindside you. Which is why the Boomer
Chicks thought it would be a good idea to
have a *backup plan*. Here's hoping you'll

never have to use it, but it's gosh darn nice to know it's there, just in case!

The Situation: You have retired but nothing seems to be working out the way you thought it would. Your happiness factor is below zero and you long to hit the reset button on your life and start all over again. But where do you begin? *What do you do?*

The Plan: Imagine that you actually *do* have to start all over again. How would you go about it? Where would you live? How would you make it on your current income? Plan out your "new" life in the most minute detail. Make a list of people you can count on to support you emotionally and consider any financial situations you might encounter. List the places where you would like to live. Then record everything in a diary (that you hide in a safe place, of course!)

Once you have a backup plan, you'll

rest easier knowing that, even if retirement life does throw you a curve, you can meet every challenge with confidence, optimism, and joy.

Now Go Have A Happy Retirement!

About the author...

Gail Mewes

When the author turned 50, she defied logic and good sense and began a six weeks, 1,300 mile odyssey with her dog, Winnie, down the Mississippi River to New Orleans in a foot pedal boat to raise money for cancer research. Along the way, she depended upon "the kindness of strangers" for food and shelter. Without a big name publicity team, her *Down The River For A Cure* campaign managed to raise over $5,000, all of which she donated to cancer research in memory of her Boomer Chick friends.

Gail and Winnie aboard the Minnow

Photo Courtesy of TheHawkeyeNews.com, Burlington, IA

Made in the USA
Middletown, DE
27 July 2019